Manku Too
More Haiku From A Man's Point Of View

Manku Too
More Haiku From A Man's Point Of View

John F. Rowles
First Edition

J4MC

J4 Music & Composition, LLC

Manku Too
More Haiku From A Man's Point Of View

J4MC

J4 Music & Composition, LLC
Herndon, VA 20170, U.S.A.
www.j4musicandcomposition.com
john@j4musicandcomposition.com

ISBN-13: 978-0-9915926-4-7
ISBN-10: 0991592646

Cover design: Kevin Richardson
Kebo Designs, LLC
http://kebodesigns.com
kebo@kebodesigns.com

Illustration: Vidya Vasudevan
http://vidyavineed.blogspot.com
vidyavineed@yahoo.com

Editing: Colleen Sproull

Acknowledgments

I would like to thank the following creative souls that contributed their time, talents, support, inspiration, and encouragement to make Manku Too happen:

Kevin Richardson, Vidya Vasudevan, and Colleen Sproull. Without all of you this book would still be just an idea instead of a reality.

To my wife Rebecca and our daughters Erica, Kadidja, and Taylor

Chapter 1
Housework

Housework will not kill
The manliness inside us
The mess is your fault

How is it that the
Laundry never ends just turn
Boxers inside out

Dishes we won't do
Paper plates do make more sense
Real easy clean up

Vacuuming is fun
Designing carpet patterns
Counts as abstract art

Carpets hold bad stains
Bad smells bad looks must discard
Hardwood cleans easy

Having carpet is
The same as having a pet
Both stink and leave stains

Without vacuuming
Don't even think of mopping
'Til the dust settles

Understanding a
Mop and bucket is futile
Let it dry and sweep

Dusting tabletops
Is a task where the effort
Surpasses the gain

Organizing stuff
Brings instant and immense joy
'Til the wife sees it

Cleaning A/C vents
How do they get so nasty
Cleaning takes all day

See the fireplace
Plenty of ashes that can
Wait until next year

All things in their place
Can anyone remember
To put things away

Wipe your nasty feet
Before coming in the house
That's what mats are for

Yes food will explode
If cooked in the microwave
Longer than normal

Cleaning microwave
After the food explosion
Goes to the culprit

Home decorating
Does not need a man's input
Why bother asking

Making the bed is
Nonsense to those of us who
Toss and turn all night

Moving furniture
An assiduous effort
By wives with ideas

A bit more over
That's too far please put it back
Let's try it again

Absent of judgment
Wall won't decorate itself
Hang it where she says

Wife has more ideas
My wallet shrinks with every
Whim there's no escape

Must all rooms be filled
There's solace in open space
She doesn't think so

The fridge is now dead
Water leaking everywhere
Repairs expensive

Dryer also dead
Piles of dirty underwear
Excessive costs loom

We need a new bed
She says with great fortitude
Budget collapses

New fixtures she said
New paint everywhere she said
Get to work she said

Cleaning the toilet
This is an effective way
To get men puking

Scrubbing shower grout
Chemicals that help clean it
Are worse than the mold

New shower curtain
Those damn clips break easily
Thwarted by plastic

Need to keep the peace
Everything must be replaced
Wifey has spoken

Sprucing up the house
Happens at the last minute
Before guests arrive

Regular housework
There's never equality
She says you do less

Purging junk from home
Decisions on sentiments
Circumvents progress

Cheap carpet runners
Placed in strategic patterns
Mitigate paw prints

Doggy brings in mud
Paw prints all over the house
Perpetual mopping

Our hardwood floors
Become a mopping nightmare
Dog shows no respect

The home of your dreams
Change everything to suit
New lifestyle wishes

More home improvements
Upscale fixtures are costly
Highway robbery

Wiped down everything
How can there be more dusting
Progress all for naught

Cleaning the toilet
We confess we made the mess
We'll cede where we peed

Clutter in the home
Her side of the room perfect
His side un-perfect

Flee the honey-dos
Harassing squirrels is more fun
Blast them all to hell

Chapter 2
Yardwork

The purpose of a
Lawn mower is to cut grass
Why can't kids learn this

Weeding is fruitless
One week later they come back
Weed killer useless

Flowerbeds only
End up as a salad bar
For furry yard beasts

Driveway cracks yield weeds
We spray pull use weed whacker
Damn things just won't die

Do not attack my
Hanging plants squirrels
Pellet gun will kill

Must clean the gutters
Heights and a shaky ladder
Becomes a deathtrap

Neighbor's yard looks great
Ours brings no competition
Brown grass brings us shame

Yardwork has its perks
Surprises on shoe bottoms
Can ruin said perks

Stay out of my mulch
Keep your ass out of my yard
Back to hell squirrels

Birds are engineers
Building nests to raise babies
Perfect cups of mud

The neighborhood cats
Roaming yards to terrorize
The @#$%ing squirrels

Buy a snow blower
Without one the sciatic
Propagates revenge

I love my chainsaw
Nothing like the feeling of
Unbridled power

Get cordless tools
But be very careful as
Wife wants ROI

No running mowers
Before 9am this causes
Rage in our neighbors

Encourage your kids
Show them the joy of yardwork
Among other chores

Four bails of straw
Cover traffic areas
Where the dog tracks mud

Chapter 3
Work

Why why why why why
In the place where most needed
Common sense dies out

No words can describe
The lack of concentration
On conference calls

Can you hear me now
A question most asked when one
Forgets she's on mute

Colleagues come up with
Ideas that can change the world
No balls to voice them

Confidence in your
Colleagues' ineptitude can
Always entertain

Divert managers
Until they give up the search
They interrupt work

Sometimes you just need
Stale cookies and some coffee
To get through the day

Analyzing facts
While trying to keep laughter
Hidden from PM

Tech specs below par
Project plan insufficient
Mission aborted

If there's any doubt
The subject matter experts
Will just pass the buck

Consultants make too much
Overpaid part-time workers
New exploited slaves

Certifications
Expensive classes proving
Participation

Careers develop
Who you know not what you know
Carries the most weight

Newest bestest plan
Will surely bring happiness
Management says so

Grant access or not
If we do can you promise
Not to screw it up

Is it impossible
To expect true agreement
Regarding projects

The warranty date
After project completed
Will be forever

We are all clueless
About current and future
State - neither will work

Blank stares everywhere
Daydreaming and killing time
Is this billable

Cubicle fodder
Packrats everywhere you look
Attack of the slovenly

Elevators stink
Perfume smoke-breath
Men's room smells better

Abbreviations
Acronyms apostrophes
Language obscurity

Conference or consultation
Replaces false memories
With new fallacies

Email and voicemail
Technology has stripped us
Of our privacy

Work home life balance
Companies espouse
Work becomes your home

Listening at work
To music you enjoy most
Will get nothing done

If there isn't time
The company won't fall down
If done tomorrow

Help us understand
Why an urgency to us
Comes from poor planning

We'll take care of it
Your urgency averted
We have thankless jobs

We all need time off
To recharge our minds and purge
All the shit at work

Taking vacation
Work will be ever watchful
Just to get called in

Distinguish people
Not those with too much but those
Who give all they got

Contemplate three walls
No fourth wall qualifies your
Cube as a sitcom

There is nothing like
The microscope of pressure
When micromanaged

Processing red tape
The cost of doing business
Plus the loss of time

Follow procedures
Dodge them when necessary
The work still gets done

Reserved spaces at
Work account for those people
Who kiss major ass

Days full of meetings
Tears up the daily routine
Disturbs your naptime

Moving up the chain
Career paths wind down the road
To oblivion

Management wanders
Gotta watch your back
Designate a sentinel

Colleagues are family
They hear the best and worst from
Just 10 feet away

Our home offices
A shrine to the company
Tethered by laptop

Tuesday or Wednesday
What day of the week is it
Damn…slept through Monday

Be conscientious
Thankful for the cleaning crew
Stop being a slob

Do you hate your job
In today's economy
You should be grateful

Entrepreneurs
Backbone of all we hold dear
American dream

Follow your passion
Doing what you love to do
Hope it has healthcare

Home from the workday
Sitting in the recliner
With beer chips and dip

Chapter 4
Men's Room

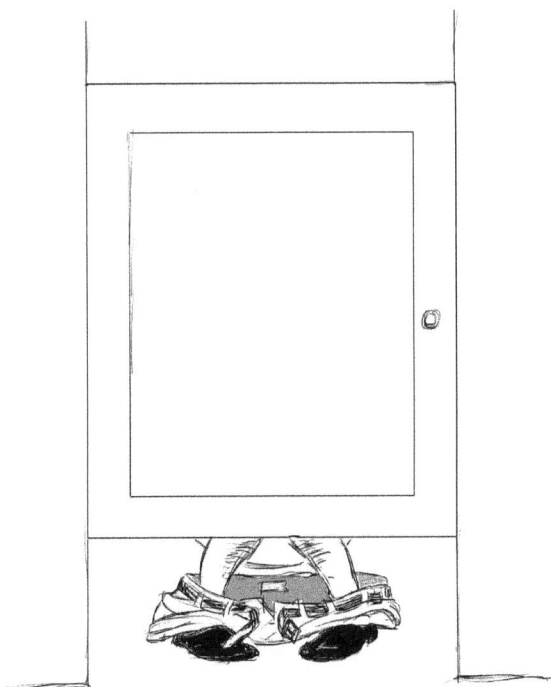

The hell that is smell
Depends on what stall you're in
Take it like a man

Getting out of bed
After a night of scarce sleep
Thanks to the bladder

Use soap and water
Germs do not discriminate
Men's room is nasty

The next stall over
Someone is creating a
Symphony of farts

Stalls in the men's room
Are stinky offices where
Best ideas are born

The drain in the floor
Not meant as a urinal
Unless stalls are full

That is not music
Coming from the other stall
Unless you're tone deaf

The restroom is closed
It knows when you have to go
That damn little sign

No true privacy
When using the stall thanks to
Bodily functions

Is the ladies room
Also a place of heinous
Odor or is it clean

Y'know just a thought
Instincts or "instinks" depends
On which stall you're in

Snoring in the stall
Gives away your location
And your work ethic

Chapter 5
Health

Smoking will kill you
Your wife will catch you at it
Her wrath is deadly

Loaded nachos taste
Like the perfect way to die
Don't skimp on the cheese

Gotta have some fudge
The fragrance of chocolate
Flying calories

Men don't do pushups
We do what's called push-aways
Unless there's dessert

As men grow older
Glasses are necessary
For shots beer and sight

Thinking of your health
You may not want that third slice
You are what you eat

Home cooking brings out
A man's inner food critic
That gives great reviews

No sense in denying
Eating the leftovers will
Score points with wifey

Watch what you eat sir
In fact watch it disappear
Should have tasted great

No body shaming
Define your thoughts of beauty
View your reflection

Eat jalapenos
You love to devour them
They love to hate you

Enormous food bowls
People ask how you eat that
One meal at a time

Running and walking
Biking and hiking 5ks
Leave it to young folks

What's good for the heart
Is a glass of wine per day
Along with nachos

French fries aren't that bad
Measure with moderation
Then ask for more

Fried foods in the South
A staple of our diet
So are heart attacks

Covered in batter
Are the delicacies of
Unhealthy eating

High cholesterol
What is LDL why care
Your family needs you

There's no replacing
Coffee with anything else
Fosters consciousness

We all should wake up
To a cup of fresh coffee
Adult breast milk

Chapter 6
Media

24/7
Broadcasting nothing but fear
Divides the masses

Radio on Earth
For those of us jailed in cars
Propaganda hell

TV violence
Marketed to the children
They are what they see

After pondering
The world seems less impressive
Media proves it

Media conscience
An oxymoron or just
Everyday morons

Lists experts make up
Don't let others think for you
It's all conjecture

Top 10s and Top 5s
Such worthless information
Make up your own list

Celebrities dodge
Jail time for media time
Money says it all

Internet foibles
Make sure to clear history
Shit can get real...fast

Social media
A place where the entire world
Became narcissists

Comedy channel
Represents journalism
Legitimately

Game shows publicize
How intelligence is used
And it's lack of use

Basic cable blues
Why do we pay for channels
We will never watch

Faux news is honest
It perfectly lampoons what
We're supposed to trust

Stare down at your hands
Smart phones do take the place of
Real interaction

Smart phones are quite smart
Gadgets that transform people
Into the undead

Apps for everything
We need an app to get back
To socializing

Phone zones not allowed
Meal time is family time
Not zombie buffet

If there is an app
To keep kids off of their phones
Please let parents know

Chapter 7
Adulthood

If YOLO is true
Maximize yourself with time
Kick ass and take names

Bucket lists are goals
Live your life to the fullest
Regret is for wimps

Squinting indicates
It's either time for new specs
Or a larger font

Middle age has pains
Popping joints crackling knees
Aging melodies

Time is contingent
On how long it takes to make
It to the bathroom

Watch movies at home
The pause button allows for
Endless bathroom breaks

Damn technology
Supposed to make life easy
Didn't quite work out

Haven't figured out
The bells and whistles pointless
Rotary phone please

Stuck in the phone zone
Try talking to each other
Old school ways work too

Remember when phones
Hung on the wall and stayed home
Good old days are gone

Dining with grand kids
Location doesn't matter
Food will start to fly

Young parents take heed
Leave the kids with a sitter
Get time for yourselves

We didn't come here
To pay for a great time out
To hear your kid scream

Often times we think
It's great having an empty nest
But still miss the kids

Family visits
We'll never get there enough
Guilt pours day and night

Ah the holidays
How much will it cost this year
Way more than last year

Time with family
Kids fall back into their roles
Parents do as well

Do not touch my stuff
One child protecting their space
From the other's germs

She's looking at me
He won't stop annoying me
More backseat bitching

Siblings do compete
Grades jobs attention and food
Struggle for power

As they get older
Children want to be your peer
They will be someday

The zeal to have kids
Young people have no idea
Of the work ahead

My children are just that
Your view of how I parent
Will get you knocked out

Potential husbands
My daughters mean more to me
Than your well-being

The street lights are on
Excuses will not save you
From a talk with Dad

Childhood was fun
Adulthood is for working
Rest when you grow old

No one can stop time
The precious moments you have
Must not be squandered

Doing while we're young
Still isn't enough of a
Deterrent for pain

As we get older
All our past desires
Are now afterthoughts

Young millenials
Entitled little snobs whom
We love and support

Feet back knee joints hurt
Need to find some painkillers
And a good cocktail

Pets bring so much love
They are the only happy
Souls to see us home

With coffee in hand
On the deck with a stout hound
The way life should be

Loyal dog at our feet
No matter how bad she stinks
She's still man's best friend

Dog barks constantly
Every little movement
Animated noise

While walking the dog
We hope she drops poop quickly
During commercials

Out of courtesy
Curb your dog pick up the poo
HOA will fine you

Arguing with kids
Is a pointless exercise
But keeps your mind sharp

Salt and pepper hair
And a widening waistline
Still play like a kid

The midlife crisis
For men it's the end of youth
Still want a hot rod

Man code 101
You own the remote control
Until she gets home

Man code 102
Don't bother with a budget
When beer is needed

Man code 103
You admit wrong-doing first
Then ask for a beer

Man code 104
Keep her happy by getting
Beer for you and her

Man code 105
It's never to late to say
I'll do it later

Man code 106
Never make it obvious
When viewing side boobs

Chapter 8
Fandom

Bandwagon jumpers
Worst example of fandom
Stay true to your team

No matter your team
No matter how bad they are
Don't change the channel

Rally towels and hats
Fans will always carry hope
Even when there's none

Excruciating
Offense and defense still suck
First round pick next year

Collegiate football
Spending all day Saturday
Ignoring yard work

Don't try explaining
The intricacies of sports
Some folks don't get it

You know it's coming
The play action pass always
Works on the goal line

Got to be a replay
No way he was out of bounds
Hometown referees

No use in screaming
The coach will screw it up
We all know better

Please fire our head coach
Offense defense special teams
Are worse than last year

Please keep our head coach
His draft picks have been genius
Playoffs here we come

Punters have merit
He's the last line of defense
Hope he can tackle

The man cave divine
Sanctuary when needed
Temples to our sports

TV size matters
Your manhood is in question
When hosting game day

A beloved team
Win or lose deserves loyal
Fan criticisms

Those fair-weather fans
Need to decide win or lose
So they can sulk too

Size really matters
TVs must show us the game
Just like being there

We all buy into
The offense and the defense
Just not the coaches

The pregame BS
Sportscasters pontificate
While we prepare snacks

Believe what you want
The South has risen again
Through college football

Basketball is on
Our team has the final shot
Pray to the sports gods

Without a jersey
You can't show true loyalty
It's bad luck if washed

Your intense game face
Bringing the A-game with you
Helps you socially

The favorite bar
Carries all the home games of
Local crappy teams

Chapter 9
Music

Studying music
Poring with contemplation
Soothing of the soul

Dulcified with jazz
Salving improvisation
Freedom of the mind

Classical music
Shoulders immense arrangement
Virtuosity

Great bass players bring
Smooth intellectual grooves
Combine peace and love

Rock and roll music
Born from so many sources
A genre stepchild

R&B music
Crosses all race barriers
Polished excellence

Country music takes
Writing from desolate farms
To America

Vinyl then 8-tracks
Cassettes CDs digital
We love our music

Despite what you think
All drummers are musicians
Stop the prejudice

Nostalgic music
Screaming guitars pounding drums
You still want to rock

No two musicians
Think alike we all must be
Ourselves while jamming

Music can soothe souls
It teaches all the subjects
True education

Not enough drummers
A band is only as good
As the timekeeper

Consider music
Melodies with consciousness
Brings love to the soul

Free mind expression
The only way to stay sane
Make true melodies

Music can't be made
Without imagination
Pour your soul in it

Corners of your soul
Desire to be filled with
Creativity

The brass trumpeting
Woodwinds dance around the scale
Strings flow through the chart

Taking from the greats
Stylistic influence
Make your sound brand new

Music of today
Is the same noise our parents
Thought of our music

Practice will get you
Nowhere without playing live
You belong on stage

Without melody
Life's footsteps take us nowhere
Roads with no music

A pair of drumsticks
In the hands of a master
Will put you in awe

Play open mic nights
Being nervous is righteous
Play it cool and jam

Marching band practice
A cadence is all we need
In the heat and snow

In charge of the stand
Page-turner is a player
To be named later

Not everyone takes
Band as seriously as you
It's their loss not yours

Practice rooms promise
Opportunity to hone
Band period songs

Unless it's blatant
On the stage audiences
Don't hear your mistakes

Even the hair bands
Deserve some recognition
Only a little

The early big bands
Standards we still play today
Never out of style

Radio has shown us
How it has segregated
Audience rhythm

Relative major
Is only three half steps from
Relative minor

Math can be explained
In a measure of music
Subject cross over

Gifted musicians
We aspire to mimic
To be great ourselves

Treble and bass clef
Different approach to the staff
The same flats and sharps

Those who play by ear
Have talent outside the book
A feel for the mind

Classically trained
Many interpretations
Praise to the masters

Watch the conductor
Your eyes must be fixated
Else there is chaos

Chapter 10
Politics

The Beltway Bandits
Marvelous examples of
Well-paid Criminals

All the talking heads
Pontificate their doctrine
Manifesting hate

The public has been
Led to the trough of falsehood
Brainwashed by the news

If politicians
Think they speak for the people
It's time to rise up

Who should we elect
Two entitled families
Shouldn't pass the crown

Rich thumb their nose at
Bottom 99%
Financial bloodshed

Political games
Elected entertainers
Circus for the world

Capitol Hill
Contains mass quantities
Of disappointment

History repeats
Live and die by the lessons
Congress never learns

Current events leave
Much for our minds to ponder
Our world needs fixing

Longing for justice
Our government is guilty
Of brokering fear

We keep electing
Left and right buffoonery
Oust all incumbents

We should all protest
Criminal politicians
Forget who hired them

Among the top minds
The most overpaid thinkers
Enter politics

Too many factions
Politics sucks out the worst
From the best of us

The House and Senate
Opinions coming up short
Of intelligence

World terrorism
International bullies
Put them in the ground

Midterm elections
The ones who screwed us at first
Come back for seconds

Senate and the House
500 and 35
Of the worst of us

Political roar
Grandstand play of loud egos
With nothing to say

Election years show
Red states blue states purple states
States of confusion

The talking pundits
Getting paid to spew bullshit
All of it nonsense

Latest breaking news
Has already been declared
An hour ago

Creative process
Stymied by terrorism
We are all Charlie

Headlines of the day
Misleading information
For suckers like us

Some speculation
Leads to cerebration
Which sounds like it hurts

Anger and yelling
Two staples seen on the news
Promulgating fear

Cable news reports
Without a doubt are written
Between commercials

Don't trust in the news
Journalists give us one view
Omitting the truth

Chapter 11
Roadku

Get off my bumper
Your lateness is not my woe
Your horn doesn't help

Driving in DC
Middle finger is ready
Going nowhere fast

Again in traffic
Stuck in a large parking lot
Really have to pee

Daily commuting
In the DMV becomes
Levy of patience

Traverse orange cones
Would love to run them over
Driving annoyance

The end of the line
Doesn't come without delays
Single tracking woes

Within the confines
Of traffic a car becomes
A road ornament

Fog fog fog fog fog
Fog fog fog fog fog fog fog
Fog fog fog fog sucks

Three and four way stops
First stop first go no one knows
Who has right of way

Don't be an asshole
Be courteous dim your lights
High beams blind people

Hearing of a crash
Whilst driving to and from work
Dictates attitudes

Again in traffic
Stuck in a large parking lot
Nothing is moving

A parking structure
Doesn't protect your car from
Weather or birdshit

When you are parking
Your SUV is not made
For compact spaces

Chapter 11
Miscellaneous

In life there are two
Sides to everything only
One is right not his

Don't be led astray
When she says let's go to lunch
Kidnapped for shopping

Fodder for the brain
Don't ask her for approval
Know she won't like it

Women change their minds
Often enough to frustrate
Temperance tested

Giving in is key
Wifey will have no issue
Making your life hell

Hunting and fishing
Necessary time for men
Don't forget the beer

Sitting in nature
Calm and quiet interludes
Until someone farts

Need no calendar
Time is not of the essence
Highlights will repeat

No need for PC
Modern day segregation
By using hyphens

Comic book heroes
Need to be responsible
To pay for damage

Haiku ain't easy
Too much thinking and counting
Head and fingers hurt

Stereotyping
Traditional gender roles
Have become passé

Sheer plagiarism
Don't believe the internet
Use books to study

Copy and paste is
No way to get through a class
Use pen and paper

College tuition
Employers don't care about
All the debt incurred

You don't need college
To increase experience
Debt isn't worth it

Beer can pop-tops
Are fatal for facial hair
Mustache misfortune

Love peanut butter
Without it empires will fall
School lunches would suck

Tonight tomorrow
Nothing guaranteed
But peanut butter

Recognizing facts
Can never convince others
Why men are always wrong

Do I look stupid
Yes your new haircut is great
Would say nothing else

Everything I learned
Saturday morning cartoons
Provided it all

The grass ain't greener
Leave one hell for another
You will soon find out

The End

The End